53 STRATEGIES TO GET MORE LISTINGS

Real Estate Agents that REALLY work

by Jason Morris

Introduction

I'm Jason Morris and I founded the Facebook group Real Estate Agents that REALLY Work. I have been in the real estate industry, actually selling real estate since 2004. In the last few years I kept looking around the industry at all of the training, classes, coaching and webinars being offered and I just was not happy with the quality of what I was seeing.

The industry has been littered with people selling training material based on certain hot buzzwords that get agents away from doing the actual stuff that makes money. I created **Real Estate Agents that REALLY Work** as a response to what I was seeing. I wanted to share real strategies and things I was personally doing to get a predictable amount of business month after month.

The business isn't really as difficult as most real estate agents seem to think it is. To make money you only have to do 2 things, either talk to buyers or talk to sellers. The problem most agents have is they don't know how to find buyers and sellers. That is why I wrote this book. I wanted to give agents ideas on how they could go and find more sellers.

Real Estate agents are not being taught ways to scale their business quickly and control their life and schedule. The best way to do that is is to build a business that is seller client heavy. Which means you need to go out and list as many properties as you can.

I put together this book from personal experience and looking at things I have done in the past and currently do that have provided me predictable sources of leads.

This book was written with the newer agent in mind and to give existing agents ideas on additional lead sources. In some states/counties/cities you may have to look for a little different process or figure out the process for your area to get the information I talk about.

These are 53 ideas and strategies to help you reach your goals. The goal of this book is to make you think creatively about where your business is coming from.

Actually the book ended up with a few more ideas than I originally planned, so I threw them in.

I wish you the best of luck building your business

Sincerely,

Jason Morris
Real Estate Agents that REALLY Work

You can join my Group here
www.facebook.com/groups/RealEstateAgentsthatREALLYwork/

Table of Contents

1. Tools you need to get started
2. Craisglist FSBOS
3. Craigslist FRBOs
4. Sphere of influence
5. Expired Listings
6. Door Knocking around just solds
7. Call Past Buyers and Sellers
8. Look up your past/current sellers in Tax records
9. Look for Small Builders
10. Landlord Evictions
11. Reo/Bank Foreclosures
12. Foreclosure Auctions
13. Door Knock Hot Neighborhoods
14. Old Expireds
15. Contact Old Short sale and REO buyers
16. Agent Referrals from Expireds
17. FSBO DAY
18. FRBO DAY
19. Old Withdrawn and Canceled Listings
20. Expired Listing from Flat Fee Companies
21. Property Tax Delinquencies
22. Property Tax Redemptions
23. List Low Priced Properties
24. Network Online with Agents

25. 3 times a day with Expireds
26. Drive Around looking for FSBOS
27. Vacant Homes
28. Zillow FSBOs
29. Zillow Make me Move
30. Probate Leads
31. Geoleads
32. Open Houses
33. Door Knock Neighborhoods
34. Home Evaluation Leads
35. Network at Local Business Events
36. Facebook buy/sell groups
37. Prospecting Building permits
38. Municipality Lis Pendens Filings
39. Property Management Company Referrals
40. Homeowner Association Referrals
41. HOA (Homeowner Association) Liens
42. Unique Selling Proposition
43. Cold Calling
44. Lot/Home Packages
45. Properties in Litigation
46. Problem Properties
47. Divorce Attorneys
48. Bankruptcy Attorneys
49. Relocation Companies
50. We Buy Houses signs
51. Cash Offer Leads
52. Short Sales
53. Land Tract Sales
54. Library Newspapers
55. Read the Newspaper
56. Local Government Meetings
57. Ask Your buyer leads
58. Signs, Business Cards etc

Tools you need to get started

Before we get started in actual strategies to get listings I wanted to layout a few tools that you are going to need. I want this book to be actionable for you and for you to be able to get the absolute most from it! To get a list of the tools I am actually using in my business today go to www.RealEstateAgentsthatREALLYwork.com .

I want to set you guys up to win so I want to make sure you have all the basic tools you need.

CRM

You need something to help you manage your database and the people you have actually talked to. You are going to generate a lot of leads using these strategies and you can't remember every person you talk to. Sometimes I can't even remember who all I talked to yesterday.

You need an easy to use CRM or database management system. You don't have to go out and get the top of the line most expensive system out there. A lot of them offer free trail periods. Take a look at them, try out a couple. Figure out which one fits your business and your needs. If it is too difficult to use, you just will not use it.

Phone

I know this seems like common sense, but sometimes its not You need a phone with unlimited talk time. I put this in here because I know a lot of agents get into the business with a lot of different expectations. You have to have a phone number that is yours and you control that is on your own plan. People will keep your phone number for years! You dont want to lose business because you used a phone line for your business cards and all your calls that is going to change in 6 months.

Computer/Laptop

I often see new agents trying to operate their entire business on their cell phone or tablet. These are great tools, but there a lot of things that wont replace having a laptop or computer. You dont need the nicest one on the market. But to effectively operate you have to have tools that make things easier. Technology is getting more advanced every day, but if you make it difficult you just won't do it.

Follow up plan

Very few times do we make 1 call, show up and close. We all get lucky and from time to time it happens, but you need to go ahead and accept that many of these strategies will take a follow up plan. This is where your CRM will be your best friend.

Pre-Listing package

If you have been to my facebook group or listened to my youtube videos, you already know, this is the #1 tool in my tool box. You can download my template at www.JasonMorrisPrelistingPackage.com. This is an outline of the basic services you are offering. Some of these strategies may require you to customize your package to fit the needs to those specific clients.

Internet

You do not have to have an amazing website and huge social media following, but you do need to make sure people can find you when they search your name in Google. There are so many scams today that people are skeptical and they should be. They have every reason to be. So you can't be a secret agent. Make sure people can find you online.

I am sure there are a lot of other things you need that I have left out. These are just the basics. You might want to listen to my podcast titled "50 things every real estate Agent needs to do" here is a link https://www.youtube.com/watch?v=7_vXqCEP2FQ

Let's get started talking about strategies you can really use to get listings with.

Craigslist FSBOs

I LOVE craigslist for sale by owners. A few years ago craigslist was a super hot lead generation source for buyer leads. It still is, you just have to work a little harder. There never seems to be as much competition as people think either. I will call craigslist FSBOs sometimes that are in hot price ranges in my market and I'm the only agent that called them.

The thing about these leads is if they are not renewed in 45 days they drop off the site completely. I chose to just print the new ones out dailey, call through them and they add them to my database. Depending on your market these people might be getting a lot of calls, however 99% of them are asking them to rent the place out, owner finance or some version of lease option.

You have to develop a system for these leads. Make sure you call, then send the pre-listing package and then follow up until the give up. The biggest challenge is, these people are probably getting a fair amount of calls. Usually you have to follow up until they have gotten tire of low ball offers and feeling like they are just spinning their wheels.

Sometimes these people do actually sell their homes. In that case you just throw the lead away and there will be a fresh new list of free FSBO leads tomorrow!

Craigslist FRBO

I figured I would get craigslist out of the way first. If you are not using it you are missing out on a fantastic free lead source!

Craigslist For Rent by Owners are great! There are a lot of management companies and apartment complexes that are using craigslist now days because they know it works, so you have to sort through those to find the true owners that are self managing.

A lot of these people are self managing because they just don't have the room between rental rates and payments to be able to afford to pay someone else to deal with it. The people in this situation are just barely hanging on to the place.

FRBOs are more long term business for me. In most market right now the rental market is moving pretty quickly. So there is a good chance by the time you get them on the phone, they have an application and a waiting list. That is ok. The strategy is not to list the property today. The strategy is to have a meaningful conversation, gather information and hopefully get an email address.

This is long term business. You want to follow up with FRBOs about once a month or a couple times a quarter. What you are waiting on is them to get tired of being a landlord. Usually this happens when a tenant is moving and they realize all the work to get it back rent ready, rents go down or just tenant problems. Most landlords are 1 eviction away from wanting to be completely done with the place.

Take these leads, put them in your CRM and follow up with them!

Sphere of Influence

We all know way more people than what we think we do. This is sort of a tricky subject. I feel like agents talk about building your sphere of influence but a lot of agents just do not get it.

If you are brand new in the business, this is going to be a lot more work for you than if you have been in the business for a while. Ive talked to a lot of agents and a lot of them are like me when I first started. I lived in an area I was brand new too. So I really did not have a sphere of influence, I didn't even know my neighbor. But you will develop one it just takes some time.

What you need to do initially is, make a list of people who live in your market that you know. Index cards work really well, a note book works well to start. Eventually you will have to migrate to a crm. To start you need a list of these people. I'm going to give you a couple of ideas on what to do with your sphere and how to stay in contact with them without spending a fortune.

I know there are a lot of programs out there a lot of you have done like an 8x8 some sort of 32 touch type of program. Some of these are really expensive and labor intensive programs and systems. You do not really need all of that now days.

The truth is most of your sphere of influence is too busy to have a 15 minute conversation with you during the day. My grandma does not even have time for that for me some days. Then, they dont look at your post card. They get a stack of junk mail every day. Sending a monthly postcard or letter to these people can be costly

You need to divide your sphere of influence up into 2 categories.
1. People you just know
2. People you know that know everybody else

Make a list of everybody, but then make you a list of the most influential ones, these are the ones you do want to call. Think of the ones that come in contact with the most people or the ones that come into contact with the most home owners. The ones that maybe work for HOA management companies, they work in the handyman or maintenance industry. Like HVAC repair people, plumbers etc. Preachers are a great one if you know anyone very active in organizations like churches, Human resources people. Basically people that come in contact with a lot of other people. These people need to be your best friends. They are going to tell a lot of people about you.

Now you can't call these people and just go "hey you know anybody selling a house? Ok Bye" You need to build relationships . Facebook is great for this, become genuinely interested in their lives. If they put pictures of a new grand kid on facebook, send them a message, call them, maybe send them a $5 gift in the mail. Don't be a stalker just acknowledge what they have going on and celebrate their successes.

If they send you a buyer or seller, invite them to lunch or do something nice for them. Do something meaningful. Facebook is so great! If you see their birthday pop up, these are the people you don't want to write on their wall, you want to call them up or send them a message and tell them happy birthday and ask how things are going. I look down through my facebook birthdays everyday looking to see if I need to call anyone or at least send them a message. Something simple like "happy birthday, I hope you have a great day! How have things been going?" It doesn't have to be a long drawn out conversation. A handwritten note works well too especially since no one does them any more.

These people, in group #1, that come in contact with a ton of people, you need to be friends with them. You can not bombard them with real estate stuff and begging for referrals. You have to build relationships

Ok now let's talk about everyone else. The person you went to highschool with that works in a factory or still waits tables at a local dinner are still important. The truth is, they come into contact with a lot of people too, they work with a lot of people.. The stay at home moms, they come in contact with other moms. These people typically have families also.

Now you are probably thinking, they already know somebody that is a realtor. That is true, but they might not remember they already know someone that sells real estate.

I'll tell you guys a story. I have a cousin that lived in New York. I see them every major holiday. Christmas, thanksgiving, all of those. I had been in the real estate business about 2 years, they decided they wanted to buy a vacation home, guess what? They didn't know I sold real estate! They bought a half a million dollar home and did not use me as their realtor. I lost a $15,000 paycheck, because I never thought to tell my family at christmas I sell real estate. My mom, brought it up to them, they said they didn't really know I sold real estate. The story gets even better. Like 5 years later they were getting a divorce, they sold the house, for about $500k. They again did not use me. I lost another $15,000 check. Six months later she is telling the story about selling the house. She said, she didn't know I was still in the business. Back then I never talked about selling real estate or the real estate industry with my family. I figured they didn't want to hear about it.

So what I am telling you, is you can't be a secret agent. I love to post funny things that happen to me during listing appointment or with clients on Facebook. It gets comments, it gets likes, but it reminds people I sell real estate.

So these random people that you know. Facebook is a great free tool for working your sphere of influence. Its one of the best CRM management tool you can have to keep up with people

Use the list feature in your facebook so put your friends, family, sphere that you want to build better relationships with into list. When you click on these list it shows you everyone that is in the list and what they posted today. It makes it really easy to click like, make a comment or send a message to someone about something significant going on in their lives. Also the more people that you interact with, the more people that see your post show up in their news feed. So when you do post something about real estate, the more people that see it.

The key to working your sphere of influence is to build relationships and keep in contact with people. You don't have to have 15 minute calls with them all. Just every so often ask how they are or what they have been up to.

Working your sphere of influence is pretty easy. Especially with Facebook notifying us of all of their big life changes and events.

I regularly get business from my sphere of influence. If developed properly this can be one of your largest lead sources.

Expired Listings

Expired listings are probably one of the most talked about lead sources on the planet! I got started calling expired listings. The reason so many agents fail when calling expireds is they just do not call enough and they give up way too easy.

The key to expired listing is using a script, following up and being consistent with your prospecting.

I talk to a lot of agents that will change scripts every week or anytime they see one get posted in a facebook group that looks more exciting. Everyone thinks their is a magic script or a magic questions. The truth is there is not. There is no secret and there isn't any magic either.

The script that works the best is the one you use over and over. Once you have been using the same script for 30, 60 or 90 days you get to a point where you know all the objections to all the questions you are asking and you know how to overcome those objects. Plus you build confidence and muscle memory, you can make small tweaks to make it fit with your own personality and local market situation.

Everytime you switch scripts you have to learn new questions and figure out how to overcome new objections.

If you stick with a script and a prospecting schedule for 90 days, your luck with expireds will change and they will get a lot easier.

Door Knocking around Just Solds

This is a great strategy to use. You ever notice how when one house goes on the market, it isn't very long until another house goes on the market down the street? Or when a house sells another goes on the market in the neighborhood. That is what you are looking for with this strategy. You are looking for the next house going on the market.

If you are a brand new agent I understand you don't have any just solds to go door knock around. That is ok, you can use just solds from your office.

Do not overcomplicate what you are doing with this, it is pretty easy. If you are just getting started you probably don't have any marketing material to leave on anyone doors or anything like that. Don't worry about that, if you are brand new, the number 1 thing you need to do is just get out there and take action. So I'm going to give you the script and everything you need to use if you don't know where to get started.

1. Get a stack of business cards and put them in your pocket.
2. Print out 100 or so 1 page MLS sheets of the just sold MLS listing with your contact information.
3. Wear comfortable shoes

Park your car somewhere out of the way. Go knock on the door. If they are home say: Hey my name is _____ I am with (realty company) we sold a home down the street at (address) (hand them the MLS sold sheet). I was wondering if you knew anyone in the neighborhood looking to sell their home? If they say "no" thank them and hand them a business card and say "if you hear of anyone could you give me a call or have them call me?". Then knock on the next door.

If they are not home, take your MLS sold sheet, fold it in half and write on the back "I'm sorry I missed you, would you like to sell your home?" then stick the MLS sheet in their door. It is really that simple and there is no need to over complicate it.

Call Past buyers and sellers

This probably seems pretty much common sense and seems like it should be a part of your sphere of influence but a lot of people leave these past clients out. Hopefully everyone is happy with your services you provided after the closing but lots of times these people fall through the crack and kind of get lost.

If you are a new agent, you might not have any past clients to call, but if you work at an office that has been there a while, they probably have a lot of these past clients. They also have a lot of agents that have moved on to other offices.

Contacting these past clients is more of a warm call, hopefully they know you or at least know your company and the brand.

In most states the broker in charge owns those transactions. You might want to talk to them and see if they have the contact information for those old past transactions.

Look up past/current sellers in tax records

This is a great strategy I figured out by accident one day. I was looking for the tax information for a property I was going to list that day and I looked up the seller in the tax records. I just happened to see where this seller owned some other property he didn't mention when I talked to him on the phone. I waited until we had all of the paperwork signed for the listing I just took, then asked about the other home I saw in the tax records. He told me how they were talking about selling it too but they just didn't know when.

I waited until we got a contract on the listing I just took, then started asking about when they wanted to sell the other property. I done 2 transactions with that 1 seller within about 3 months.

The point of this story is sometimes the clients just don't mention they have other property they are thinking about selling. It just doesn't come up.

Look up your current and past sellers in the tax records and see if they have anything else they might be willing to sell. It would be a good idea to look up buyers in the tax records too. If they are buying a new house, they might not want or need to hang on to another property they have.

Look for Small builders

This is a great strategy in any market. Now you might be saying to yourself that these people already have agents they are working with and you can not contact them. That is correct if you are a REALTOR you are not suppose to contact other agents clients. But you are not contacting them about the homes they currently have on the market, you are contacting them about future business.

What I am calling a small builder is someone without a sales team or office building less than 10 to 15 homes a year. They may not even have an office or more than 1 administration person.

Working with builders is more about building a relationship. The building business is a place where money is made by counting your pennies and saving money wherever you can. It is also a business where they have to sell to survive. If they can't sell a house, they can't go build a new house. Every builder wants to build 1 or 2 more homes a year.

The easiest place to find a list of small builders is just to look up your home builder's association website and typically the will have a list of builder, their contact information and their website. The second place is to use Google and do some searches for home builders. You can also drive around and when you see a house under construction, stop and ask someone "who is the builder? Can I get him number?". A lot of times they will just give you a name and probably a phone number.

You want to look at these potential clients, not as 1 time clients but as continuous ongoing business accounts. Finding one or two small builders could add 5 to 10 maybe even 20 or more transactions to your business each year.

This lead source is going to be all about building a relationship with them and waiting for the opportunity to get a chance to work with them. Keep in mind, they are also people that are constantly being contacted with somebody trying to sell them something. They have sub contractors calling, building supply vendors calling and probably a list of other people we don't even know about.

For a lot of agents getting one builder client relationship could change their entire business.

Landlord Evictions

First of all, you are not contacting the tenant. That probably isn't going to help you very much. Plus they are in the middle of, in some cases, a stressful legal action. Calling the owners of properties that are currently having tenants evicted is probably one of the most underused listing strategies out there.

If you have ever worked as a property manager or owned rental property you know that this whole process is very frustrating. In most cases the person being evicted is being evicted for non-payment. In many markets the reason the property owner is renting the home is because they couldn't sell it a few years ago and they couldn't afford for it to sit empty. So at this point many of these owners are just tired of dealing with it and they want it to go away.

Here is why most agents are not contacting these property owners. The information is kind of hard to get. Evictions are a legal action and they are public record. You may have to go down to the courthouse or call a title company and figure out how you can get a list of these properties where evictions are in process right now. If you county has court cases online, you might can look them up there. You can get eviction information, it will take you making some calls and figuring out where to get it from.

I recommend calling and sending mail to the property owner while the eviction is still going on. Technically they can't really sell the home in the middle of an eviction, the tenant probably will not cooperate with showing. That has been my experience. What you can do is get a headstart on any other competing agents. These properties typically will not be for sale by owner or anything while the eviction is going on. If you wait to contact the property owner until the eviction is over, then you might have other competition from other agents or they have already made a decision on the future of the property.

For contact information you can look up the owner's mailing address in the tax records. The owners phone number you can outsource these number lookups or use some free sources like whitepages.com and do reverse number lookups.

You will need to do a combination of mail and calls, it may be difficult to find phone numbers for many of these property owners. If you are persistent this is a great source of business. You will need to set up a system to easily get the eviction information from the courthouse and then easily get contact information for the property owner.

REO/Bank foreclosures

No matter what you believe the economy is going to do, there will be another recession at some point in the future. The real estate market is always going to have ups and downs. There will always be foreclosures.

I have worked with banks selling foreclosures before. Most banks in today's financial world are selling properties through servicing companies. Not many of them are actually handling their own foreclosures directly.

Like I mentioned with small builders, having a bank that is providing you an extra 10 to 20 transactions a year can really change yourself business. In many case you will apply to a lot of banks and asset management companies. You typically have to do an actual application. Many times you get put on a list and you basically have to wait until someone quits or messes up. You are looking for the opportunity to be given a chance.

A lot of asset management companies will ask for you to do BPO (Broker Price Opinions). Often times the banks assigning REO/foreclosure listings are not going to offer you payment for this service. So be careful that you are not being used.

Some agents love doing REO foreclosure work with banks and there is a lot of opportunity to work with banks. There is a lot of paperwork involved. Often times you will have to do weekly inspections and monthly market reports on properties. With many banks you will be required to change the locks, have electricity turned on, even hire vendors to clean the property up. Typically this cost comes out of your pocket and you get reimbursed.

I do not discourage anyone from going after this business, but it can be very labor intensive.

To get a list of asset management companies there are a lot of companies that will sell you a list, for under $100. You can also join several REO Networks and associations that can give you more information on what companies to contact.

Foreclosure Auctions

I have done a lot of business from foreclosure auctions. It is not from representing clients at the auctions themselves, because as far as I know most foreclosure auctions will not pay a real estate commission. Ive done business with the people I have met there.

In most states foreclosures are still auctioned off at the courthouse. Each state and county may be a little different but you can just call the courthouse or look online and find out when and where these auctions are held.

Going to 1 auction might not help you much. But after you have went to several you will start noticing a lot of the same people are at every auction. These people are your true investors and property flippers. Some may have real estate licenses but that is ok. If you can build relationships with these people, you could gain a steady client and a client that is always looking for deals.

In most states you can even get a list of the auction results. In my area it is easier to pay for it than to research the results myself. If I have a client looking for a deal, the auction results are the first place I look. A lot of times these buyers are willing to take a small profit the day after the auction and pay a real estate commission but still leave some money on the table for somebody else to make some money.

Auctions are one of the best places you can go to meet true investors that have access to money. If you are wanting to list the home they are selling you need to have a plan and be able to perform for them. Many of the clients you will meet they at auctions are in positions where they have to sell one to buy another one. A lot of the ones I meet, this is their livelihood, it isn't a part time way to make extra cash.

Door Knock Hot neighborhoods

This strategy is pretty simple. You need to have some sort of material to leave behind. A market report of the neighborhood, a newsletter or some personal marketing material.

The idea is pretty simple, look up neighborhoods in your market or around where you live. Find the ones with high turn over. I would look for neighborhoods with around 150 homes that have an 8% or better turn over rate. That way you know there are about 12 homes selling a year in the community. It averages out to a deal a month.

Door knocking neighborhoods is a great way to farm an area. It will be a lot more effective than mail. Lets face it we are all desensitized to mail. We all get so much junk mail that a lot of it just goes in the trash without ever being opened. If someone leaves something in your door you look at it.

The key to this is going to be repetition. Going every month and putting out information with your name and contact information on it. After a few months, everyone will know who you are. This is a great place to network, a lot of the people there are going to have houses to sell in the near future or have a house they need to sell right now.

Old Expireds

One thing I have learned is once an expired is over about 90 days old, agents seem to forget about them. The number of calls that seller is getting will go down dramatically. Calling expireds that are over 90 days old are great, but the ones with little to no competition are the ones that are a year or two old. A lot of these people ended up renting the home or doing something different with it. It does not mean they don't still want to sell it, it just means they got tired of waiting. The good thing is, depending on the market you are in, if there house was on the market 3 years ago they can probably get more for it today.

When talking to agents, the biggest problem most of them have is they don't know where to get the old number from. Personally I use Redx and they offer a service that will go back and look these numbers up. Plus if you tell them I sent you, they have some special deals. If you are going to call older expireds, you are going to have to have a system that will make it easy for you to get numbers. If it is too difficult, you are not going to do it.

Contact old Short Sale and REO buyers

Chances are, if someone bought a short sale or REO property 1 year ago to 5 or 6 years ago, (depending on the market) they probably have a ton of equity.

Now you might be thinking they already have an agent or know an agent, but chances are that agent abandoned them as soon as the home was closed.

Not everyone keeps up with the market like you and I do, but these people may not know their home could be worth 10%, 20% or more than what they paid for it. Plus if it is a primary residence and they have lived in it for 2 years, they might not have to pay taxes on their gain (check with an accountant or tax professional).

This property value increase for most of our country could be a huge windfall!

The leads you get from calling these people are typically going to be long term leads that you may have to nurture for a little while.

Once you find one that may be interested in selling, they need to be added to your database and called on a regular schedule.

Agent referrals from expireds

You ever had that client that just would not listen to anything you said!? You showed them the comps, you begged and pleaded and nothing would happen. Then all of a sudden they listed with another agent and done exactly what you said and the home was under contract in 2 weeks.

That is so frustrating! Other agents are going through that too and properties are expiring off MLS because of it. The other thing is, with cell phones and all of the other technology people have it is tough to figure out how to contact sellers sometimes. Even with the best expired services and on a great day, you are not going to get correct, accurate numbers for more than 50% of the expired listing out there.

But I know who has that contact information, the agent that listing expired from. Now you say "wouldn't that agent want to re-list it?". Maybe they do, but sometimes the seller just wants a change and wants to go with someone different.

Calling or email agents regularly asking for referrals can be a huge business. Like everything in sales business it is a numbers game. Not every agent is going to run go get their past client's contact information and hand it over to you.

Once you have went through all of the new expired listings, go through and email the agents of listings you did not get numbers for.

This is a fantastic source of listings that is oftentimes overlooked. I have used this strategy in the past myself. At the peak of the short sale boom, I was regularly helping other agents negotiate short sales for their clients. Other agents didn't want to do it, I personally didn't mind doing the extra paperwork.

Pre-foreclosures

This is a lead source I get asked about a lot from agents all over the country. I don't really see where there is near as much competition as you would think. Most agents are too lazy to do the extra work to go after a lead source like this one.

The first question we need to answer is, what is exactly is a pre-foreclosure? In most states once someone is behind on payments, usually 3 payments, the bank will file a Lis Pendens. This is basically a notice that foreclosure is coming. There are several services you can buy regularly updated lists and get the information as soon as the notice is filed. You can also get the list from a title company or you can research it at the courthouse. I would recommend buying the data, looking it up yourself is going to be labor intensive.

The biggest problem I have had in the past is I would get the information before the property owner was served the foreclosure notice. So I would call and they would have no idea they were getting foreclosed on.

You have to be very careful with these particular leads and sometimes follow up for a few weeks. Working with this type of lead source can be difficult, many of them will be in denial at first that they are losing their home.

You can not call them and use a script that is basically "Hey I saw you were getting foreclosed on? Want to sell?" it isn't going to go over very well.

Sometimes you will have to follow up for a few weeks, send a couple of mail pieces. Once someone is over 90 days past due, the chances of them getting caught up are very slim. There are a lot of programs available still to modify their mortgages to get caught up.

If they are upside down, a short sale could be a great option for them. MakeHomeAffordable.gov is still offering program like HAFA for moving allowances and a lot of banks that took bail out money are still having to offer short sale incentives.

There will be that odd person every now and then that just decides they are going to not pay and just live there until the bank takes it from them. I have had people call me just a few days before their home is going to auction and they want to get it on the market. If they contact the bank, there is a good chance they can get it pulled from the auction and get the opportunity to sell it themselves. Technically the bank does not want their home, they just want their money.

If their home is about to be auctioned off, they can sign a listing appointment, get it on MLS, contact their bank and have a good chance of getting it pulled from the auction.

To list these properties you are going to have to call and send mail. You will need a solid follow up plan that last for 12 to 15 weeks. You have to follow up and wait for reality to set in for a lot of these home owners.

The first calls you make to them just asking simple questions, do not mention the pending foreclosure. It is my experience they property owner will become very defensive and tell you that is a mistake or they have gotten it worked out. Introduce yourself and ask "I was calling to see if you would be interested in selling your home or do you know anyone in your neighborhood looking to sell?" The first call for me is a typical script you would use phone farming a neighborhood.

Sometimes they will ask how you got their information, at that point I would tell them. Be almost brutally honest with them "I got your name and address because your home is on the list to be foreclosed on."

With any mailers you have, you need a strong call to action. I'm not a big fan of mail, but for these types of leads, sometimes it is the only way to get in contact with the owner.

This is a great source of what could potentially be motivated sellers that often times have no choice but to sell. Often times pre-foreclosures are possibly upside down. In that case I immediately ask them if they would like to just get out from under the property. Many times a short sale is the best option for these home owners with no equity.

Old FSBO Day

These are my favorite days. Old FSBO day. What I do is subscribe to a for sale by owner gathering service. I also print out FSBOs every day from craisglist, zillow, facebook groups and anywhere else I can possibly find them.

The easiest thing to do is have them in a format or a database so you can just upload them into a dialer and wait for someone to answer the phone. A lot of the time FSBOs will give up after a little while. They still want to sell, but they have expired off craigslist, they are old on zillow and agents have kind of quit calling.

I will call/contact these home owners until their phone is disconnected, their email doesn't work, they tell me it is sold or they just tell me dont call back.

Those old lists of FSBO are gold! Most of the ad have the owners cell phone number and often their email address.

I typically have a day or two a month that I only contact FSBOs. It forces you to go back through these old leads and I always set 3 or 4 appointments.

This does a couple of things for me.
#1 it forces me to follow up with old leads I never talked to.

#2 it forces me to follow up with old leads I just forgot to call back

If you are not scheduling 1 day a month to do nothing but call old FSBO leads you are missing out on a lot of money. This strategy alone could bring you a couple of extra listings a month.

FRBO Day

Just like the FSBOs I plan 1 day a month to call old For Rent by Owners. Just like I mentioned in one of the earlier sections of this book, I never throw these leads away.

Everytime I get a FRBO that I talk to on the phone, I add them to my database. Once a month, I try to contact as many people as I can front that database.

I typically plan this somewhere between the 15th and the 20th of the month. In most markets rent is typically due on the first of the month and late on the 5th. Now this could vary state to state. You should contact your local magistrate's office to see what the eviction timeline looks like in your state. Here in South Carolina rent is typically due on the 1st and later after the 5th, then once the tenant is 5 days late the landlord can start eviction. Typically if the landlord is having a tenant issue or thinking about an eviction, this reality is setting in around the 15th of the month.

What you are looking for is just that tired landlord. The person that just don't want to deal with tenants any more, they are barely breaking even on payments and they just want to get out from under the place.

The typical script you use is pretty simple. Introduce yourself and just ask if they are thinking about selling their property. Then just let them talk. If they say no, just move on to the next number and call them back in a month or two.

Old Withdrawn and canceled listings

Old listings that have been canceled and withdrawn are often just forgotten about. I have noticed talking to real estate agents all across the country, not a lot of agents call these listings.

A lot of the time these listings are taken off the market for so many reasons. It could be something as simple as they decided not to sell. It could also be they just decided not to sell at that moment.

By old withdrawns, I'm talking about the ones that are 4 to 6 months old or older. I have noticed that sometimes even the old listing agent forgot about these people, they didn't even go pick up their sign or lockbox.

The thing about these home sellers is the older ones are often better than the brand new ones. Typically they pulled the property off the market for a reason, a few months have passed and often that reason is gone and they still would like to sell. The other thing is, maybe these sellers had a problem and you can become a problem solver and help them.

I call these leads and treat them the same as I do an older expired listing.

Listing that expired from Flat Fee Companies

These are great leads to call and watch for. In most markets flat fee companies will require you to contact the seller directly. They only offer a very limited service which is usually just a few pictures and inputting the property into MLS.

A lot of the time expired services will not get phone numbers for these expired listings because everybody has cell phones now days.

The good news is if you look in the agent to agent remarks or showing instructions, the flat fee company probably left the seller name, cell phone number and even the email address still in the listing.

These sellers often listed with a flat fee company because they didn't think they needed a full service company and they were trying to money. Expect commission conversations and often times not very much equity.

Property Tax Delinquencies

Property tax notices come out once a year. When those tax bills are not paid those tax liens get auctioned off. Check your state but in the State of South Carolina if you buy a tax lien you have to wait a year to be able to redeem it and actually take possession of the property.

You can get a list of all of the properties and owners that had properties that got auctioned off. These people are often in one of a few situations. They possibly can't afford the taxes or they just didn't get the tax bill and they forgot about it.

Usually you can get a list of the properties that are up for auction by just going to the courthouse All of this is public information. You can also contact a title company and get this list. You will need to also get the address to where the property tax bill is being sent. Often times the seller might not actually live or get mail at the property.

To get phone numbers you will have to do some work. You can do searches on website like whitepages.com or hire someone to do the research for you from a website like upwork.com.

Typically you will not get a whole lot of phone numbers for these sellers on your own. Depending on the size of your county, this list could be enormous. You might want to go through it or have an administration person go through it and take out the properties you are not interested in.

The listing strategy will not have much competition. Most agents will not do the work required to get all of the data needed to pursue these listings on a larger scale. You are probably going to have to expect to spend money on a mail campaign.

Tax Deed Redemptions

These leads like the Tax notices are going to require work, but you are going to probably be the only agent in your market going after them. You are going to need to do some research and learn the process in your county/state. Each state is different. In the state of South Carolina someone will go bid on a property at a tax sale, then 12 months later they can redeem that tax lien for a tax deed.

The person that purchased the tax lien often times will do it just because they will get interest on the tax lien that is pretty much a guarantee of anywhere from 8% to 12% or more depending on the state you are in. Worse case they end up getting the property. Typically when they end up with the property they got a pretty good deal on it. Sometimes they got it for pennies on the dollar.

A tax deed in most states is not like a regular deed. In most states to get a clear title they new property owner will have to go through a process to completely clear off junior liens.

If you want to go after these types of listings you should contact a few attorneys you work with and ask questions about the process.

To get a list of the deeds that have been redeemed through the tax sale process you can talk to your local title company and ask if they can do the research for you. Of course you can always go to the courthouse yourself and look for these new tax deeds, but it may very time consuming.

After you get the information on the process and the tax deed list, now comes contacting the new owners. You are going to find out pretty quickly there are 2 very different types of people that end up with these deeds.

#1 The first person is the one that invested in some tax deeds for the return and got really lucky and ended up with a tax deed. They do not have a clue what to do since they got the deed. This is the first time it has ever happened. You need to be the expert in this situation or at least be able to refer them to the expert.

#2 The second type of person is someone who does this professionally. They go to the tax lien auctions with intentions to end up with the property. They are typically very experienced and have a variety of exit strategies. This could be a great on going client.

These listings would be looked at by a lot of agents as problem listings. If you no the process to get a clean title and the process for the tax lien holder to acquire the title, it can be a great source of business with very little competition.

List Low priced properties

Now I know a lot of agents say things like "I don't want to list properties under ____" or "I work too hard for such little commission. So what happens is the low priced FSBOs and the low price expireds get over looked by agents calling them.

Here is the thing about these listings, often these sellers know their property is low priced and an average commission is not going to be much money.

What you need to do is establish a minimum listing side commission for your business. Come up with an amount that you feel is fair and that you can justify. Personally I like a flat fee minimum on the commission side of these small transactions. If you remember in real estate licensing classes all commission are negotiable. You or your company set their own commission or fee schedule. You can charge as much or as little as you would like as long as the market will bear it.

I consciously call lower priced listing. Once reason is they get a lot of activity and the often sell. The second reason is no one else is calling them. On days I am going through a little slump or trying hard to get my numbers I will sort my data base and expireds to call a lot of lower priced properties.

Typically they are easy listings to get. As long as you can justify your fees you can get higher than your market average to take these listings.

Network Online with Agents

A lot of agents discount the idea of referral partners. Most of you reading this book know me from my group Real Estate Agents that REALLY work. The things most agents do not know about me is I'm willing to share or help just about anyone willing to help themselves.

I network like crazy through facebook with agents outside of my market are. I am in a big second home market, I get referrals like crazy from Facebook. Facebook groups are the easiest place to share information and stand out. I have an abundance mindset. I started sharing things I was doing in facebook groups and quickly started getting known as an expert by agents.

It wasn't long until when agents would post in referral groups needing an agent in Myrtle Beach, SC and other agents would tag me in their post. I have an army of agents tagging me in referral post. Then on top of it, I have a ton of agents who refer clients directly to me.

I would suggest if you are not looking for this type of business you should start, a referral lead is the highest quality lead you can get. All of you have to do is start participating. It does not have to be a big time commitment either, just plan about 15 or 20 minutes a day to scroll through a few groups and comment on post, ask questions or post a questions. The more you are willing to give the more this strategy will give you back.

Try 3 times a day with expireds.

Depending on the size of your market and the number of expired listings you have, pick your area wisely.

Look through the expireds for listings in your target area that you did not get a phone number for with the expired service you are subscribed to. Chances are if you are using a high quality service, if you didn't get their phone number nobody else did either.

Go door knock on this person's home. Go in the morning, around noon and then the afternoon until you catch them at home. It should be pretty easy to figure out if the home is occupied.

Chances are if you are having trouble getting in contact with them, other agents in your market are too. With cell phones and different cell phone plans, some people are constantly changing numbers. Not everyone is like real estate agents, I've had the same number since I first started in the business and I have no intentions of changing it. Other people that are not self employed change their phone number whenever they change their service.

Door knocking expireds without phone numbers could be huge for your business.

Make sure when you knock on their door that you have something that you can leave behind. A flyer or a door hanger works very well.

Drive around looking for FSBOs

This is one of my best sources for business. When I'm going to or from a listing appointment or just driving home or whatever I'm doing, I do not pass a FSBO sign without getting the address and phone number off the sign.

I will hold up traffic to get a FSBO number off a sign. The best ones are the ones in the back of a neighborhood. Chances are if all they done is put a sign up in their yard, they haven't gotten many calls and not many agents are calling them. Especially if it is a road that doesn't get much traffic.

I plan time before or after every appointment to drive around the neighborhood looking for FSBO signs.

If I have time, I will park in the driveway and call while i'm sitting in front of the house. I tell the seller "I am driving around in the area looking for houses for sale". I'm very blunt and bold with that statement also.

Some days I have scheduled time just to drive around areas looking for signs. Paying attention and looking for FSBO signs are a fantastic source of business. Every time you see one of those signs and you just pass by without getting the number you are throwing away money.

Look for vacant homes

This is very similar to the FSBO strategy but it takes a little more work. When you are going to and from listing appointments and other daily travels. Look for homes that are clearly vacant. Usually the big sign is the grass and yard is very unkept.

Writing down the address and look up who the owner is. You can use a website like whitepages.com to try to locate a phone number for the owner.

You can send these property owners mailers. Sometimes it can be hard to track these property owners down. Usually you can knock on a neighbor's door and ask if they know who owns the home or how to get in contact with them. Sometimes the neighbor will just give you a phone number.

Zillow FSBOs

If you have not noticed I love any FSBO leads. How much easier can it get. These people are sticking signs up in their front yard and putting ads on line that basically say "Hey I want to sell my house and I do not have a real estate agent".

Zillow FSBOs are very similar to craigslist FSBO. These are typically people who are just trying to sell themselves to save commissions or they just don't want to deal with a real estate agent yet. It could be a list of reason though.

With FSBO you need to be very direct and follow up like crazy. In my market Zillow FSBOs seem to be the most heavily called FSBOs. Often times you will have to make 3 to 12 follow up calls or more to get the listing.

You need to set yourself up a system to get these leads into your CRM and a follow up system. Most of the time they have put their cell phone number on the ad. If I can't get them on the phone i text them.

A lot of the FSBO gathering services grab the zillow FSBO listings. I still check them regularly, sometimes they miss one or there is one on the outskirts of my market that will not get picked up by their service.

Zillow Make me Move

If you look around on Zillow you will see a section with listings that are marked "make me move". I thought these were important enough to give them their own section.

Often times these are people that for whatever reason took the time to actually go on the website and enter information and list a "make me move" price.

So just by seeing their home listed you know they have made an effort to at least think about selling.

I often find these sellers are in the early stages of thinking about selling or they are waiting for something to happen to put their home on the market. For example maybe they are getting a promotion at work or they are building a house. It could be a variety of reasons that are toying with the idea of selling.

Call them and ask about the home. Worst case add them to your database and follow up in a month or so. I treat them the same way I do FSBO.

Some FSBO gathering services include Zillow Make me move listings and some do not.

Probate Leads

Probate is always very interesting to me. I have done a lot of probate and estate transactions but it has never been something I have focused on. Often times I have found these sort of transactions calling FSBOs.

For those of you that do not know what probate is, it is the process that an estate has to go through to be closed to ensure there are no other claims against the deceased person's property and assets.

Estates that are in the probate process are public record. There are services that you can use to gather these leads for you.

Often times the hard part is tracking down the executor of the estate. This is typically the person or persons that has the authority to make decisions on behalf of the deceased person's estate.

The best situation you can have is all of the heirs of the estate are on the same page as far as what they need to do with the estate. The worst case is you have heirs who are all fighting over what they think should be done or how much a property is worth. The executor of the estate is the person with the authority to be able to make decisions though.

Sometimes finding the executor of the estate is difficult because they do not normally live at the property. Depending on where your data is coming from the probate information will have an address for contacting the estate representative in it.

Networking with attorneys are a great source of referral business for these types of leads also. If you are thinking about pursuing this type of business, do some research and educate yourself on the process in your state.

GeoLeads

Contacting homeowners around Just Listed/Just Solds

This is a fantastic lead source. You ever notice how one house sells then another one right down the street goes on the market. What is happening is that home owner down the has been thinking about selling or sees the neighbor's house sells and thinks it's a good time for them to sell too.

The strategy is easy, you can make calls around your listings that just sold, your office's listings that just sold or around listings that just sold in MLS.

The script is pretty easy. You just call everyone in the neighborhood and say, "hello my name is _____ I am with (realty company). We (if it was your listing or your office's listing) just sold a home down the street from yours, would you be interested in selling yours? If they say no, ask "do you know anyone in the community that may be interested in selling?".

Be ready with community information or just sold info. Ask if they would be interested in you keeping them up to date with what recently sold. Ask for their email address to add to your database or crm.

This is a very simple process. A lot of agents will greatly over complicate it.

Open Houses

A lot of agents do not like to do open houses. They can be a ton of work but they can also be a great source of leads. With a successful open house you can't start working the day of the open house, it starts days before.

The best strategy I have used is about a week before the open house I would send out a mail piece to the neighborhood. What I found that worked the best was a large over sized post card. Something that would really stick out. We are so desensitized to junk mail, it makes it hard to really grab attention. The small post cards do not really grab attention.

Then the day before the open house go out to the neighborhood with the same post cards or a flyer, knock on all of the doors inviting them to your open house. If they aren't home stick the flyer in the door. Then I went ahead and stuck out an open house sign in front of the house with a flyer taped to it with the open house times.

The day of the open house I would put out 12 to 15 open house signs. I would use them as directional signs and put them out at the intersection in the neighborhood and all the way out to a main road.

I would also tie helium filled balloons on them, that way nobody misses them.

After that you just open the door to the house and wait. Make sure you have a sign in sheet that includes a place for their name, email, phone number and address.

You may have a few buyers come in here and there, but a lot of what you will have come in is nosey neighbors. You get to meet them face to face. Some of them will want to sell or they are thinking about it, some of them are just being nosey. Ask them all if they know anyone wanting to sell. After you do this a few times in a neighborhood with different house, send out some mail pieces and make some calls to the whole neighborhood, it won't be long and you will be a celebrity there. Everyone will know you.

Door Knock neighborhoods
(Farming)

This is different that door knocking around just listeds and just solds. With this strategy you are doing more face to face farming, you are going out to neighborhoods and meeting the residence face to face. Knocking on people's doors is going to be a time consuming process. I would not pick random neighborhoods or just develop a mindset that you are just going to knock on them all.

I would do some research in the area that you work, look for the neighborhoods and areas with at least 150 homes and an 8% turn over ratio. That means there is one sale a month to be had in the neighborhood. This doesn't mean you are going to get that one sale a month, but it isn't unreasonable to think that you could get 20% to 25% of the sales in the neighborhood.

With that success ratio you would get 2 to 3 a year from that area. Multiply that times doing 10 neighborhoods. That is 20 to 30 listing transactions a year.

The key with this will be repetition. Pick an area where you can door knock once a month. After a few months people will know you. You can also add calling and mail if you really want to saturate that area.

A farm area of 1500 homes at an 8% turn over is 120 listing a year. Start small and build. This is a long term strategy.

Facebook/google Home Evaluation ads

A few years ago these ads were very popular. What do is pay for traffic from websites like Facebook or Google and drive traffic to a website that gives a free home evaluation.

There a lot of landing page companies that specialize in creating landing pages to convert this type of internet traffic.

This particular strategy is difficult to write about because it is always changing. After a few weeks of running ads and tweaking them, you will be able to figure out what your average cost per lead is. Then after 30 to 60 days you can figure out what your conversion ratios are and exactly how much it cost you to list a property.

Once you have done enough ads and went on enough appointments and you have a cost per listing taken, you can work on scaling this strategy as high as you want.

The thing to be careful about is you always have to monitor ad cost and cost per conversion. The google and Facebook algorithms are always changing. Stuff that worked a month ago might not work at all today. When you find something that works, scale quickly and get the most out of it that you can. It will not last forever.

Network at Local Events

Networking is a strategy most of us never do this enough. It is so easy to say we are going to that Chamber of Commerce event, them completely bailout at the last minute. Using those types of business networking events is a great source of business and building referral partners.

They key is to actually keep up with the people you meet and build a relationship. It is a lot more work than just exchanging business cards, smiling and walking away.

You need to set up a system. You need a script or dialogue that you follow asking them about their business when you meet. When you walk away, makes some notes on the back of their business card so you don't forget details about them.

The next day send them an email or a text. Ask them more questions about their business, friend them on facebook, become genuinely interested in what they have going on.

After over 12 years in the real estate business, one thing I have learned is everyone knows someone looking to buy, sell or rent. You just have to build trust and build a relationship for them to feel comfortable recommending you.

Facebook buy/sell groups and Market place

Much like craigslist, its easy to figure out who wants to sell their home in these groups. They are the ones posting picture of house and details along with a price.

There is not near as many agents calling these fsbos as you would think. Most of them you can send a message and they will respond back with their phone number. They are typically easy prospects too, you already know what friends you have in common and a little bit about them.

Much like craigslist, a lot of the people responding to craigslist ads are looking for rentals or rent to own and owner financing. Even if the seller could do one of these options, the person inquiring doesn't have much for a down payment.

On facebook, the longer the ad stays up and no one comments on it the further it goes down the page. Some of these groups are so large that after a couple days with no comments, the seller's ad is almost impossible to find.

I make it a habit to scroll through these groups once a day, sometimes more if I am bored. I don't typically get a lot of leads from these groups, but I get high quality FSBOs. I send a simple message to start "What is the best number to call you about the home for sale?"

Don't over complicate this system. You may only get a few good prospects a month, but its free and doesn't take much time out of your day. Most of us are going to be on Facebook anyway.

Prospecting Building Permits

If you haven't noticed yet, there are a lot of free leads hanging around the court houses and in the public filings. This isn't the last strategy in the book that includes going to the court house.

Your court house tracks the monthly building permits that are issued and applied for. You are not looking for the owner of the property, you are looking for small to medium size builders that are actually building.

A lot of these permits will be builders building for a true end user, some of these will be builders or investors building homes to sell. Either way, networking with these builders can be a great source of ongoing business. Actually you can build an entire business around working with small builders.

If you are going to pursue this area of the real estate business, I would plan out what services you are going to offer them. The key idea to remember is they are business that have a lot of overhead, a ton of subcontractors/employees and they have to keep selling to keep everybody working.

You will need to meet and plan on building long term relationships with these people. Many small builders don't have big show rooms or marketing departments. They need real estate agents they can trust to help them sell more homes.

These are clients that could potentially transform your business. One builder, building 15 to 20 homes a year for most agents would completely change their business. Possibly even put them in a situation where they need to hire an admin or another agent to help them.

Municipality Lis Pendens Filings

First I want to explain what this is. These are problem filings that are also public record. This is where someone has violated an ordinance within a town or city.

Most towns and cities have ordinances that all property owners have to follow. If they dont the town basically sues them or starts levying fines. Each state and township is different. You may have to do some research to figure out what the customs are in your area. However, most of these violations and fines are public record.

Depending on your city, this could be a gold mine. Figuring out problems is a gold mine in the real estate industry. Most real estate agents are just too lazy to figure things out. Typically most people within your local government are helpful.

Most of these filings will be for building code violations or just violations where the property is not being kept up.

What happens a lot of the time is someone moves away, they get old, they lose their job or they have some random issue and they just don't have the money to keep up the property, now the city wants to charge them for it. In most areas if it bad enough or goes on long enough the city can condemn the property. No one really wants to deal with their property getting condemned. These are typically pretty motivated sellers. You have to do some homework to track them down if they don't live in the home. I have found people often by just asking a neighbor.

Even if they property is condemned, there i someone that is willing to purchase it and work through getting it back up to code so it is liveable.

Some of these filings are just people trying to get around the system by adding a deck or something random and not pulling a permit. But even in those cases, you never know the situation until you ask.

Property Management Company Referrals

This is an excellent source of business. Depending on your state, many property management company rent out property but do not sell property.

These companies can be fantastic referral partners. Research who they are, set up a meeting and see how you can work together with them. Often times we get overpriced sellers that need to do something. Some property management companies can even pay referrals.

Homeowner association (HOA) Management companies

These are also amazing referral partners to find. A lot of agents do not ever think about these HOA contacts as referral partners. Often times you can not do much for them, but you can get rid of headaches. They can not give you a list of homeowners that are behind on HOA fees, it is against the fair debt collection act. However they can pass your contact information to that person.

If you combine this strategy along with some of the previous strategies like door knocking, phone calls etc. You will be the superstar real estate agent in the community.

The HOA manager knows and probably interacts with every person in the neighborhood on a regular basis. Building a relationship with this person could potentially lead to a tremendous amount of business.

HOA (homeowner Association) Liens

I felt like this would be a good place for this strategy. You can't network with every HOA manager in your market, if you are in a big market there are just too many. But you can go to the courthouse or talk to your title rep about pulling you a list of current HOA liens.

An Hoa lien is a lot like a foreclosure, it can actually lead to foreclosure in most states. Once a homeowner is 3 payments or more behind the HOA can file foreclosure just like a bank can, they are typically a junior lien holder behind taxes and the mortgage, in most states. Once this starts, the bank can also file foreclosure, because they have the right to protect their position. Anyway, it can potentially be a mess for a homeowner to deal with.

Many times before a property owner starts missing mortgage payments, they will stop paying HOA payments. Typically because it isn't filed on their credit and the HOA is a little slower to file foreclosure.

These leads are very much like the pre-foreclosure leads. They are in denial and require you to just keep following up.

You can not call them and say "hey I see where you are not paying your HOA fees? Want to sell?". That is not going to go over well.

I have been to auction before where I have seen the HOA foreclose on properties and the seller wouldn't have a mortgage on it at all. They just fell on hard times and couldn't pay it.

These leads are just like pre-foreclosures, they are going to require consistent, ongoing follow up.

Unique Selling Proposition

Advertising a Unique Selling Proposition is a great way to generate business. For those of you that do not know what it is, a unique selling proposition is a unique offer that is eliminates objections. For example "Your home sold in 90 days or I will buy it" is a popular one. Also "Your home sold in 90 days or I will pay you $500 (any dollar amount)" is common.

It is typically a headline in an ad or mailer that will generate some sort of response. You can get creative with your offer and then put it on everything or offer it to just certain communities you are farming. You can also also put a timeframe on on it, where they must list by (enter a date).

Look at the common objections you are getting in your market from sellers and build your proposition around your common objections.

Cold Calling

This is truly just a numbers game. It is going to be a lot easier for you to take your database and use a dialer to call. I would suggest targeting specific areas and calling back through them regularly.

But the idea is pretty basic, if you call and talk to enough people somebody will want to sell their house or they will know someone that wants to sell.

This is a strategy that is going to be long term. You will pick up a lot of people that might not want to sell today but they are thinking about selling in the future. You have to add them to your crm and just keep following up with them, sending them mail or email until they get ready to do something. Hopefully you have made enough of an impression that they will immediately think of you when they think about what agent are they going to use.

Lot/Home Packages

One of the earlier strategies was to contact builders who are pulling permits and actually building homes. This is a strategy you can use with them.

Lot listings are typically the easiest listings to get. Most agents do not really go after them because often times a lot by itself is a low price point and they are not going to make much money just selling a home lot.

What you can do is list a lot of lots, during the listing process you can talk to your lot owners about marketing their property 2 different ways. The first way is just traditionally as just a lot. The second way is with a lot home package. Many builders are happy to take a look at the lot and give you a home plan and pricing you can put on MLS and market.

If you get a contract and pre-sell the home to be built, the lot is normally paid for and then construction starts. There is no risk to the lot owner and the builder will have a contract before construction even starts. It is a win-win-win. Plus depending on how you structure your listing agreements you can get paid both sides on the lot purchase and get paid on the home/lot package again. The commission agreement for the lot and the lot/home package is separate. So you end up getting paid 3 times on one transaction.

I know I have made this seem very simple in this section, these transactions can be very time consuming. You will want to make sure the builder has systems in place to handle pre-selling homes.

Look for properties in Litigation

So much money can be be made in these situation. If you are in a large market, especially with a lot of condos, litigation with the previous developer or HOA is pretty common. Most agents agents will avoid it. Many believe rumors about no financing or a variety of random things.

All law suits and litigation filings are on file at the courthouse. You can go down and get a copy or just read through them. Some are interesting reading. Some will be just frivolous nonsense. If you can learn how to overcome these issues in your market, talk intelligently with homeowners about the issues they are facing you can build a lot of trust. You should always avoid giving legal advice. One of the easiest things is being able to suggest financing solutions for them to sell their properties.

There is all sorts of other litigation and lawsuit issues. It could be partners filling what is called a partition of sale, meaning one partner wants to sell and the other does not. These transactions go to public auction and do not really get a whole lot of bidders in most cases.

If you want to look at getting this sort of business, you will need to really educate yourself. You should make sure you have an attorney or legal service you can call and ask questions.

Problem Properties

As real estate agents we should constantly be curious and anything unusual we should ask "what is going on there". We should also get really good and tracking people down and finding people. Anytime you see a home that looks like there is a problem going on, that is a potential listing.

We are all in one of 3 place, we just got through a problem, we are in the middle of one or we have a problem coming up we don't know about yet. Property sellers are no different.

When you drive through a neighborhood and see an abandoned house write down the address. If you see a home that looks like it was under construction and it stopped, write down the address. Anything that looks unusual get in the habit of writing down the address and researching who owns it.

You may want to just do something as simple as adding the address to your database and putting them on your mailing list.

Facebook Networking (with out of area real estate agents)

For anyone of you reading this that knows me, you probably know that I believe in abundance. If you are a member of my facebook group "Real Estate Agents that REALLY work" you also know that I dont mind sharing everything I'm doing that works.

One thing I do that consistently gets me a few referrals a month is I network with other agents. I will typically respond quickly to any request for help that I get from agents outside my area or even agents inside my market.

The more you share in real estate agent groups and the more active you are in groups, the more agents will know you. Spend a few minutes here and there getting to know them, asking them questions etc.

Make videos, share information, offer help, other agents will remember you. When you do something cool, talk about it. If someone else is doing something cool ask them about it.

It amazes me some weeks how many referrals I will get from other real estate agents that come through facebook. Make it a practice to share information and participate.

Divorce Attorneys

Divorce Attorneys can be a fantastic source of business. Many times they are representing a client and fighting a bitter battle that it does not matter what happens, but no one will be happy. There are often times property may be involved.

You will want to find an attorney that you can build a long term relationship with. Offer to do a broker price opinion for free at the same standard you would do for a bank. Which is a very detailed CMA.

If you are going to focus on this type of business, you need to have some marketing material you can drop by the Law offices regularly, say hello to the staff and drop off business cards, brochures etc. It also doesn't hurt if you buy the office lunch every now and them or bring something special by when you drop off brochures.

You want to be the person they all think of when they have a client mentioning they want or need to sell. This is a relationship you will have to continuously nurture. Most agents are not very good at nurturing referral relationships.

Bankruptcy Attorneys

This is a referral channel just like Divorce Attorneys. Just going and meeting them one time probably will not bring you any business. However building a relationship could bring you a lot of business over time.

It may take several months to get the first referrals. This is a long term strategy that you can just add into your business day. Schedule drop bys while you are in the area. You don't have to stay long, maybe 15 minutes.

Relocation Companies

If you spend some time researching you can find a lot of relocation companies that do real estate agent referrals. Typically these companies have been hired by corporations to assist their employees with moving to a new area.

These companies will often want you to meet certain qualifications or will be affiliated with certain franchises.

If you live in a larger metropolitan area this could be a tremendous source of business. The business you get from these relocation companies can be expensive. Many of them charge from 30% to 50% referrals.

We Buy Houses

It does not matter what market you are in, you have saw the "We buy Houses" signs that are at intersections every now and then. Most of these guys are property wholesalers. They are just trying to get a home under contract and then trying to flip it.

A lot of the time, they regularly get leads that the seller just don't want to sell for the price they are willing to pay.

Many of these guys are in the business of just buying, selling or flipping. They could be a great source of deals for some of your investor clients. If these guys are just wholesaling properties there won't be much opportunity to list their deals but they are a great source for undermarket properties you can make a commission on and have a good chance of listing when your investor client puts it back on the market.

What you really want is to offer to pull comparables, offer help to these people in exchange for them sending you the home leads where the seller is looking for a price closer to retail value.

This is a relationship you can build over time. A lot of agents don't feel like these people are serious buyers/sellers but they are marketing and looking for the same people real estate agents are. The difference is, they don't have to follow the rules we do and they can pass along potential clients.

Cash offer Leads

There are a number of websites that offer these kind of leads. Basically it is a marketing company that has a network of websites that offer to purchase homes for cash. These are fantastic leads for real estate agents.

You can go to my youtube channel and get a better idea of how these leads work and the scripts you should follow .

https://www.youtube.com/channel/UCFNjkAnZ7IkNygNa723qZ2g/

Search for my videos with "zbuyer" in the title. You can build a whole business around this lead source.

Short Sales

You wouldn't believe it, but a lot of agents still avoid short sales. There are nothing like they were around 2009-2010. Most of the big banks have a formal process now days and make it a very easy process. The truth is, banks do not want to foreclose.

If you have not ever done a short sale, you need to educate yourself some. Bank of America has their full process and all of their paperwork online. So do a lot of other banks. There are a few extra forms you have to do and a short sale transaction will take a little long than a traditional sale.

I list everyone I come across. I often look at them as guaranteed sales. It is going to be a well priced listing, where the seller knows they are not going to walk away with any money, so they are usually not very emotionally attached to it.

To really capitalize on short sale, you need to make it known that you actively work on short sales. Tell agents in your market that you will pay a referral. I have gotten tons of referrals from local agents for short sales, even short sold some of their personal homes. The transaction has to be arms length, so they can't list a short sale for a family member.

One question I always ask FSBO and Expireds that are just crazy over priced is "are you just trying to get out from under this house?". If they say yes, I start talking about what a short sale is.

For newer agents that don't know what a short sale is, it is where the seller owes more on the property than what the property is worth. When the market goes down short sales are more common than they are right now. They will come back when the market cools off.

Land Tract Sales

In more metropolitan areas there are not as many opportunities to list larger tracts of land. The truth is, for most agents, once they got out of the licensing classes they didn't feel like there was anything left to learn. In reality, we never can stop learning.

Some of the largest agents in the country, we will probably never hear their names because they specialize in large land sales. There isn't a lot of competition in this area of the business and most of the competition I have met are older men that are not very tech savvy.

Finding a tract of land, looking at the zoning and putting a preliminary plan or projection together is a skill set most agent do not have and there is not many places to find training material. However If it is smaller and in rural areas, you can go down to the court house and talk to someone about what can be done with the current zoning. Then you can figure out if the price or value makes sense.

Just like there are not many agents with this skill set, there are not many buyers looking to develop land. Most of them are pretty analytical. Its not like selling a home, where someone will buy something and because they love the kitchen they will pay a little more. Land tract sales and land development is very cut and dry, either it is or it isn't.

Library Newspapers

This may surprise some people but newspapers can be a great source of FSBOs. There are not FSBO ads like there use to be, but they are still in there. If you go to your local library, they will typically have 6 months worth of your local newspapers in their archives. Take a pen and paper so you can write them down. Typically these are not very internet savvy sellers. Once the newspaper ad ran out they may have just given up.

This is a great source to find an almost untapped source of FSBOs and FRBOs.

Newspaper articles

Believe it or not but keeping up with current developments and events can give you a whole brand new source of leads. In our area we had some small canals that the local city decided to dredge and do an assessment to the home owners that surrounded these canals. This assessment was going to over $10,000. So it was going to be substantial. Many homeowners didn't agree with it or didn't have the money, so they decided to sell.

What for local news stories and developments in your market. Many agents don't pay attention to these things and completely miss them. In situations like I just mentioned, having a huge bill looming is tremendous motivation to sell for some people. Tax increases can be the same way.

Also road widening projects and projects in the path of improvement. Some people don't want to live around the construction or might feel like it is a time to cash in. Looking for these developments can be huge marketing opportunities.

Local Government meetings

When a property is getting re-zones, something is being re-developed and it is serious, before construction starts, plans have to be approved by local government. You can often meet the developers and other people involved in projects.

This is a great place to find out information that will often not be in the newspapers. You get to meet the players in your community. Typically a lot of the people at these meetings are pretty influential. All of these meetings are open to the public.

Concerned homeowners often show up to these meetings also. You can learn a lot and meet a lot of people. You can build a large stream of brokerage income by showing up at these meetings and planning your prospecting around development that is going on in your area.

Ask your buyer leads

Often times when someone is looking to buy a house, they might need to sell a house. People are always looking to move up or down or just somewhere different. If they are moving from a different market, you can get paid on a referral to an agent in that other market.

It is really simple, just ask "Do you have to sell another home before you can buy?" or "do you have another home to sell?".

Do not over complicate it.

Signs, Business Cards etc

I saved this one until last. I felt like it was a given. Make sure you have your own signs, business cards and other stuff with your contact information. I often get calls from people saying things like "hey I saw you sold my neighbors house, I want to sell mine". It doesn't happen all the time, but it happens.

If you don't have your owns signs, with your number that rings to you on it, you are missing out on business.

Closing

I hope you have found this book very useful. Please go to Amazon and leave me a positive review it you did. You can also join my Facebook Group Real Estate Agents that REALLY work and look for me on Youtube.

Jason Morris

www.ingramcontent.com/pod-product-compliance
Lightning Source LLC
Chambersburg PA
CBHW070139210526
45170CB00014B/1635